SpringerBriefs in Economics

Kobe University Social Science Research Series

The Kobe University Social Science Research Series has been established as a subseries of the SpringerBrief in Economics Series, but in fact this exciting interdisciplinary collection encompasses scholarly research not only in the economics but also in law, political science, business and management, accounting, international relations, and other subdisciplines within the social sciences. As a national university with a special strength in the social sciences, Kobe University actively promotes interdisciplinary research. This series is not limited only to research emerging from Kobe University's faculties of social sciences but also welcomes cross-disciplinary research that integrates studies in the arts and sciences.

Kobe University, founded in 1902, is the second oldest national higher education institution for commerce in Japan and is now a preeminent institution for social science research and education in the country. Currently, the social sciences section includes four faculties — Law, Economics, Business Administration, and International Cooperation Studies — and the Research Institute for Economics and Business Administration (RIEB). There are some 230-plus researchers who belong to these faculties and conduct joint research through the Center for Social Systems Innovation and the Organization for Advanced and Integrated Research, Kobe University. This book series comprises academic works by researchers in the social sciences at Kobe University as well as their collaborators at affiliated institutions, Kobe University alumni and their colleagues, and renowned scholars from around the world who have worked with academic staff at Kobe University. Although traditionally the research of Japanese scholars has been publicized mainly in the Japanese language, Kobe University strives to promote publication and dissemination of works in English in order to further contribute to the global academic community.

More information about this subseries at https://link.springer.com/bookseries/15423

Tomomi Miyazaki · Masayuki Tamaoka ·
Ayu Tomita · Keigo Kameda · Akihiro Kawase ·
Katsuyoshi Nakazawa · Hiroyuki Ono ·
Naoko Yokoyama

Tax Morale and Tax Resistance

Evidence from an Internet Survey in Japan

Springer

Tomomi Miyazaki
Graduate School of Economics
Kobe University
Kobe, Hyogo, Japan

Masayuki Tamaoka
Graduate School of Economics
Kobe University
Kobe, Hyogo, Japan

Ayu Tomita
Graduate School of Economics
Kobe University
Kobe, Hyogo, Japan

Keigo Kameda
School of Policy Studies
Kwansei Gakuin University
Sanda, Hyogo, Japan

Akihiro Kawase
Faculty of Economics
Toyo University
Bunkyo-ku, Tokyo, Japan

Katsuyoshi Nakazawa
Faculty of Economics
Toyo University
Bunkyo-ku, Tokyo, Japan

Hiroyuki Ono
Faculty of Economics
Toyo University
Bunkyo-ku, Tokyo, Japan

Naoko Yokoyama
Faculty of Economics
Osaka Sangyo University
Daito, Osaka, Japan

ISSN 2191-5504 ISSN 2191-5512 (electronic)
SpringerBriefs in Economics
ISSN 2520-1697 ISSN 2520-1700 (electronic)
Kobe University Social Science Research Series
ISBN 978-981-19-0477-6 ISBN 978-981-19-0478-3 (eBook)
https://doi.org/10.1007/978-981-19-0478-3

This Springer imprint is published by the registered company Springer Nature Singapore Pte Ltd.
The registered company address is: 152 Beach Road, #21-01/04 Gateway East, Singapore 189721, Singapore

Preface

Taxpayers in Japan are often described as being very resistant to tax increases, especially consumption tax increases. Indeed, the former Prime Minister, Masayoshi Ohira, who first mentioned the necessity for taxes on a broad range of consumption goods, lost the snap general election. Meanwhile, the cabinet of former prime minister, Sosuke Uno, lost the Upper House election right after introducing the consumption tax—this was the first time that opposition parties won the majority of the Upper House since the foundation of the Liberal Democratic Party. These facts indicate that tax resistance (i.e., as per Schmölders's [1965] definition, psychological resistance to tax payment) may be strong in Japan.

Although many studies on consumption tax have been done in Japan, attention has recently moved to the topics such as consumer psychology, tax consciousness, tax morale, etc. For example, when it comes to consumer psychology, Ishida and Nakazono (2020) examined the "salient effects" of Chetty et al. (2009) by focusing on the total amount display system, which requires prices to include consumption tax. Regarding tax morale, the World Value Survey (WVS), a famous attitude questionnaire conducted around the globe, reports that Japanese citizens demonstrate a high tax morale.

The previous information suggests that while taxpayers in Japan resist tax increases, their non-pecuniary motivation for tax compliance is high. Although these are established facts about taxpayers in Japan, to the best of our knowledge, few attitude questionnaires for Japanese citizens simultaneously focus on tax hikes and tax compliance. Therefore, as parts of a project supported by a Grant-in-Aid for Scientific Research, we conducted two surveys in 2019 and 2020 to examine the two aforementioned established facts and related topics among taxpayers in Japan.

This book provides background information and basic descriptive statistics from our Internet surveys in Japan. The first survey was implemented in August 2019. We conducted a follow-up survey in 2020 to check for changes in opinion after the consumption tax hike in October 2019. These two surveys address important topics on tax and fiscal policies, such as tax morale and tax compliance, opinions on the Japanese consumption tax hike in October 2019 and the effects of debt accumulation on consumption.

We strived to address some of the problems inherent to the Internet survey. The first concern regards representativeness. We confirmed the representativeness of residential areas and household structure using the National Census. Moreover, all respondents were randomly chosen.

In this book, we focus on tax morale and the consumption tax hike. The summary statistics indicate that tax morale is high in Japan, which is consistent with the WVS. However, half of the first survey respondents opposed the consumption tax hike from 8% to 10%. Further, about 60% of respondents stated that their "ideal" consumption tax rate is less than 10%. We confirmed this in the second survey, which did not give some respondents information on the size of government debt outstanding.

The correlation matrix for the relevant questions reveals an insignificant relationship between tax morale and the indicators regarding trust in politicians and government. What is more, we found a slightly positive relationship between tax morale and social norms or a sense of sin. Thus, the source of the high tax morale of the Japanese people can partly be explained by their motivation to abide by rules or social norms.

Regarding tax resistance, we found a slightly negative relationship between resistance to the consumption tax hike and trust in government. This implies that political distrust may cultivate resistance to further tax hikes.

We realize the necessity for further econometric exercises. As an overture to further studies, this book introduces all our questionnaires and provides a brief outlook for the survey.

Kobe, Japan Tomomi Miyazaki
Kobe, Japan Masayuki Tamaoka
Kobe, Japan Ayu Tomita
Sanda, Japan Keigo Kameda
Bunkyo-ku, Japan Akihiro Kawase
Bunkyo-ku, Japan Katsuyoshi Nakazawa
Bunkyo-ku, Japan Hiroyuki Ono
Daito, Japan Naoko Yokoyama

Acknowledgments Some analyses in this book are based on "Consumption Tax Hike, Tax Morale, and Tax Resistance: Taxpayer Paradox in Japan," published in the Public Choice Studies No. 73. The authors are grateful to an anonymous referee, Nobuo Akai, Yoshihide Fujioka, Junya Hamaaki, Masayoshi Hayashi, Bernd Hayo, Takayuki Nago, Haruo Kondoh, Kazuaki Sato, Masaaki Suzuki, Takashi Shimuzu, Kentaro Tachi, Toshiyuki Uemura and Kazufumi Yugami for their insightful comments and suggestions. This work was financially supported by the Japan Society for the Promotion of Science (Grant-in-Aid for Scientific Research #16H03637 and #18H00868). The usual disclaimer applies.

References

Chetty R, Looney A, Kroft K (2009) Salience and taxation: theory and evidence. Am Econ Rev 99(4):1145–1177

Ishida S, Nakazono Y (2020) The salient effect: evidence from the consumption tax hike in Japan. A paper presented at the Japanese Economic Association 2020 Spring Meeting

Schmölders G (1965) Finanzpolitik, Zwite Auflage, Springer-Verlag

Contents

Chapter 1
Introduction

This book provides background information and basic descriptive statistics from our Internet surveys in Japan. The surveys were implemented in August 2019 and July 2020 as parts of a project supported by a Grant-in-Aid for Scientific Research. These two surveys address important topics on tax and fiscal policies, such as tax morale and tax compliance, opinions on the Japanese consumption tax hike in October 2019, and the effects of debt accumulation on consumption, etc.

This study reports results related to tax morale and opinions on the consumption tax hike. The summary statistics indicate that while tax morale is high in Japan, half of the respondents oppose the consumption tax hike from 8 to 10%. Furthermore, the "ideal" consumption tax rate for most was less than 10% in both surveys, suggesting that Japanese taxpayers are very resistant to tax payment. Although the correlation between some answers is weak, the source of tax resistance can be attributed to distrust of politicians and the central government.

The remainder of this paper is organized as follows. Chapter 2 provides the background information on the Japanese consumption tax hike in October 2019 and related policies. Chapter 3 presents the survey design. Chapter 4 reports parts of the summary statistics on tax morale, tax compliance, and attitude toward consumption tax hikes. Chapter 5 concludes the study.

T. Miyazaki et al., *Tax Morale and Tax Resistance*, Kobe University Social Science Research Series, https://doi.org/10.1007/978-981-19-0478-3_1

Chapter 2
A Brief Look at Japan's October 2019 Consumption Tax Hike

2.1 Overview of Japan's Consumption Tax System

As shown in some textbooks, such as Gruber (2019), five common types of taxes encompass taxes on earnings (or payroll tax), individual annual income, corporate income, wealth, and consumption. A consumption tax levied on a specific good is an excise tax. Consumption tax in Japan is not an excise tax; it is imposed on a broad range of consumption goods. The Ministry of Finance, Japan (hereafter the MOF), declares that "consumption tax is levied widely and fairly on consumption in general."[1]

The Japanese government founded its current consumption tax system in April 1989 by repealing the excise tax imposed on luxury goods. The consumption tax rate was 3% initially, which increased to 5% in April 1997 and 8% in April 2014.

The consumption tax in Japan is a principal source of revenue for the government. Figure 2.1 shows the general account revenue, equivalent to the revenue of the central government in Japan. Consumption tax revenue accounts for 19.5% of the central government's total revenue, almost the same proportion as income tax revenue.[2] In this regard, consumption tax is a crucial determinant of the size of the government budget in Japan.

---

[1] Please refer to https://www.mof.go.jp/english/tax_policy/publication/tax007/e_06.pdf.

[2] Readers may think that the consumption tax rate in Japan (10%) is relatively low compared to the share of consumption tax revenue to the total (19.5% as shown in Fig. 2.1). For example, the tax rate and share in Germany are 19% and 24%, respectively. However, by considering the difference in the VAT revenue ratio (0.57 and 0.72 in Germany and Japan, respectively), the difference is reduced to large extent. Considering Fig. 2.1 and the revenue shares in Germany (24%) and Japan (19.5%), we can compute as follows:

(Japan) $19.5/(10 * 0.72) = 2.708$.

(Germany) $24/(19 * 0.57) = 2.216$.

For the VAT revenue rate, see the below resource:

https://www.oecd.org/tax/consumption/consumption-tax-trends-germany.pdf.

https://www.oecd.org/tax/consumption/consumption-tax-trends-japan.pdf.

T. Miyazaki et al., *Tax Morale and Tax Resistance*, Kobe University Social Science Research Series, https://doi.org/10.1007/978-981-19-0478-3_2

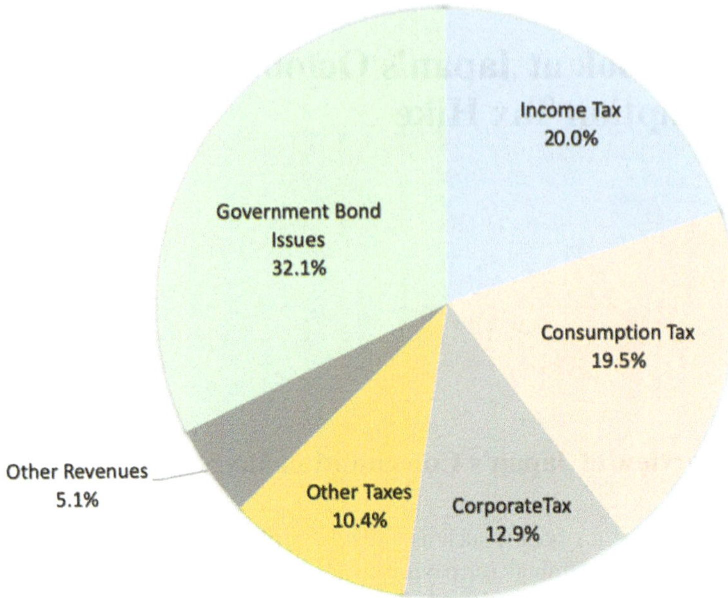

Fig. 2.1 Composition of Japan's general revenue account (FY 2019). *Source* The website of the Ministry of Finance Japan

Meanwhile, Japan's consumption tax is similar to a value-added tax (VAT) adopted in many European countries, imposed at each production stage on the value added to the good. Under the Japanese system, producers are also bound to pay a consumption tax at each stage. Therefore, the Organization for Economic Co-operation and Development (OECD) classifies Japan's consumption tax as VAT.

Figure 2.2 compares the VAT revenue per gross domestic product (GDP) among OECD countries. Japan's VAT revenue per GDP was 12.8% in 2018, lower than the OECD average. Therefore, Japanese taxpayers' VAT burden is smaller than that of other countries, whereas consumption tax is a primary source of government revenue for the Japanese central government.

2.2 Background of the Consumption Tax Hike

Figure 2.1 shows that the Japanese government relies heavily on government bonds. Over the last three decades, no country has been more overwhelmed by enormous government debt than Japan. The central government has run a budget deficit since the early 1990s. As shown in Fig. 2.3, the general government's gross debt-to-GDP ratio reached 226.5% in 2019; this ratio is the highest among OECD countries and more than double the average of the countries listed in Fig. 2.3.

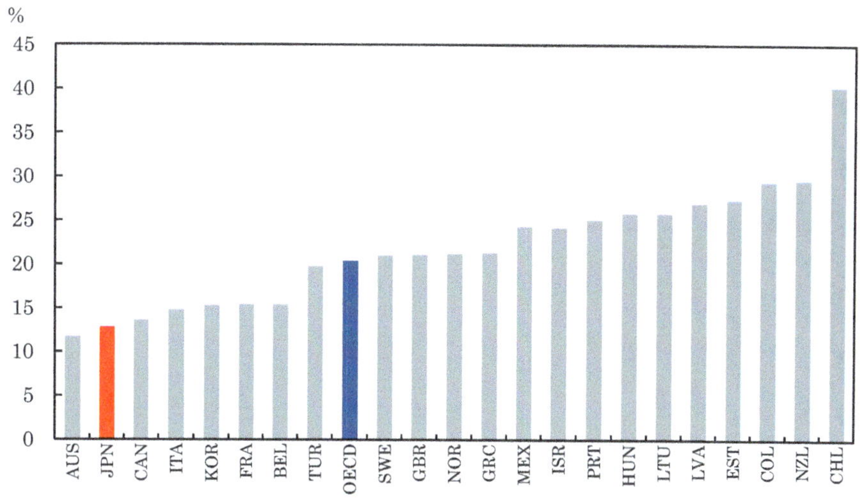

Fig. 2.2 International comparison of value-added taxes as a percentage of total tax revenue in 2018. *Source* Consumption Tax Trends 2020, OECD. Data was obtained from https://doi.org/10.1787/888934219850

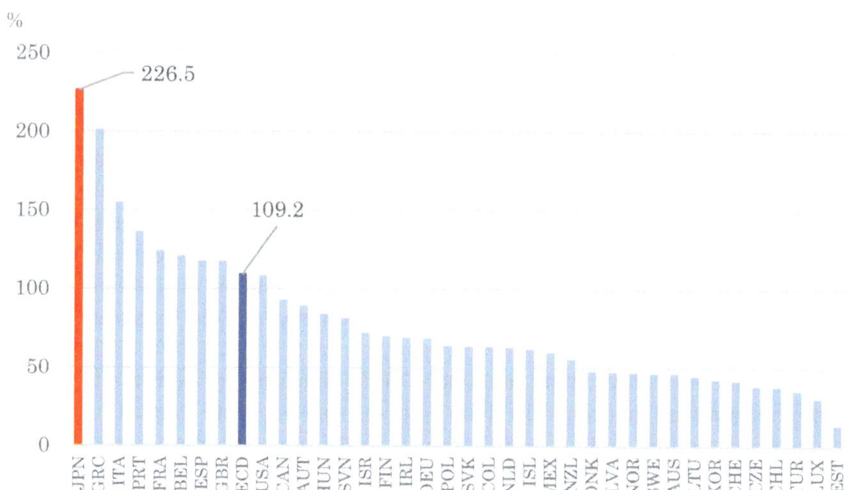

Fig. 2.3 General government gross debt as a percentage of GDP, as of 2019. *Source* Government at a Glance 2021, OECD. Data was obtained from the website https://doi.org/10.1787/888934256767

An increase in social security expenses in accordance with aging is a major cause of fiscal deterioration in Japan. According to Fig. 2.4, the central government's social security expenditures have been continuously rising, amounting to nearly 6% of GDP in FY 2016, almost double the figure in the late 1990s. Given this situation,

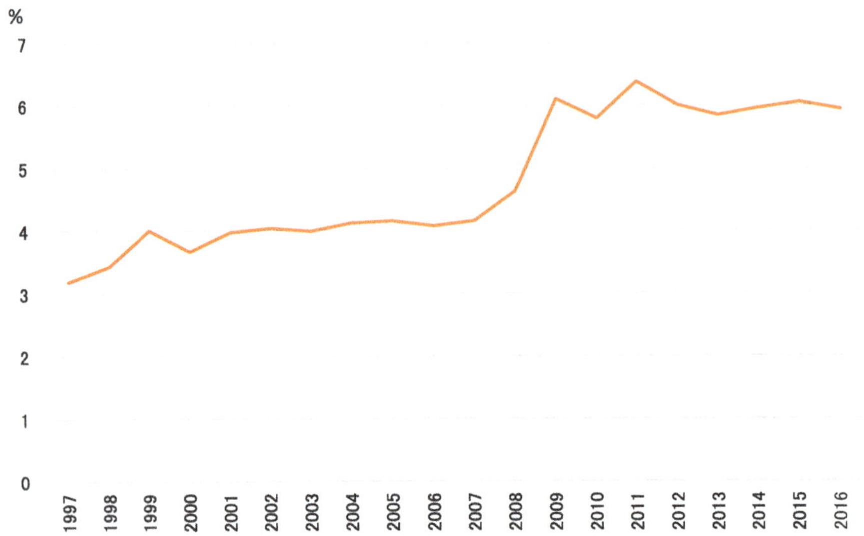

Fig. 2.4 Movement of social security related expenditure in the central government budget in Japan as a percentage of GDP. *Source* The website of the Ministry of Finance, Japan

the MOF underscores the necessity of securing stable revenue for an aging society. Theoretically, since a lump-sum tax cannot be fully used in practice, taxing income, consumption, or assets should be considered viable options. Taxes on consumption are less distortive than other taxes, such as labor and capital income taxes.[3] In this respect, the consumption tax hike is justifiable.

The Japanese government recently increased the consumption tax rate to tackle the upsurge in social security expenditures. As noted earlier, the tax hike from 5 to 8% was done in April 2014. Moreover, the government implemented a second increase in October of 2019. Following the earlier argument, the government showed that the increased consumption tax revenue should be earmarked for social security expenditures.[4]

Meanwhile, the government introduced policy measures to curb the burden on taxpayers in a way that may also help smooth business cycle fluctuations. While private consumption plummeted in response to the previous consumption tax rate increases, as shown in Cashin and Unayama (2016), the Japanese government did not take any measures to bolster private consumption or investment.[5] Policy measures were implemented in October 2019 based upon these past lessons.

[3] For more details, please see also Auerbach and Kotlikoff (1987), Hansen and Imrohoroglu (2016), and Kobayashi and Ueda (2021).

[4] For more details, please see https://www.mof.go.jp/english/tax_policy/publication/tax009/e_all.pdf.

[5] The growth rate of private consumption was −2.6% in the first quarter of 1997, when the consumption tax rate increased to 5% from 3%. Likewise, it was −4.9% in the first quarter of 2014, when the Japanese government conducted the second consumption tax hike.

First, the Japanese government offers premium gift certificates for households with children aged between 0 and 3, low-income earners, and households with a low public pension for half a year. Second, if consumers make purchases with a credit card or electronic money, they will be eligible for a 5% rebate. The government also introduced a dual tax rate system for consumption tax: a reduced rate of 8% for necessary items and a standard rate of 10%.[6] The government aims to mitigate the regressivity of VAT, as in the case of several other countries, but this was not adopted in Japan until the October 2019 tax hike.[7]

References

Auerbach A, Kotlikoff L (1987) Dynamic fiscal policy. Cambridge University Press, Cambridge

Cashin D, Unayama T (2016) The impact of a permanent income shock on consumption: evidence from Japan's 2014 VAT rate increase. RIETI discussion paper series 16–E–052

Gruber J (2019) Public finance and public policy, 6th edn. Worth Publishers, New York

Hansen G, Imrohoroglu S (2016) Fiscal reform and government debt in Japan: a neoclassical perspective. Rev Econ Dyn 21:201–224

Kobayashi K, Ueda K (2021) Secular stagnation and low interest rates under the fear of a government debt crisis. J Money Credit Bank Forthcoming

Tamaoka T (1994) The regressiveness of a value added tax: tax credit method and subtraction method: a Japanese case. Fiscal Stud 15(2):57–73

[6] The MOF uses the description "reduced tax rate system for consumption tax" to specify the system. For example, please also see the webpage: https://www.mof.go.jp/english/tax_policy/consumption_tax/index.html.

[7] Regarding the regressivity of VAT, please also see Tamaoka (1994).

Chapter 3
Survey Design

3.1 The Attitude of the Japanese People Toward Tax Policy and Survey Design

Paying tax is stipulated as a civic duty in Article 30 of the Constitution of Japan. Nevertheless, Japanese constituents have a negative impression on consumption tax and have resisted its increase and introduction. Tamaoka (1994) points out that special interest groups—especially small traders, retailers, and even consumers—recalcitrantly resisted the consumption tax in the 1980s. Further, most Japanese administrations that proposed or implemented a consumption tax hike lost national elections. According to many newspaper polls, more than half of respondents oppose further consumption tax hikes. These facts suggest that tax resistance (i.e., as per Schmölders's (1965) definition, psychological resistance against tax payments) is likely to be high in Japan.

Meanwhile, "tax morale," as defined by Luttmer and Singhal (2014), captures non-pecuniary motivations for tax compliance as well as factors that fall outside the standard, expected utility framework, such as intrinsic motivation, including shame-based guilt and trust in government. Here, there is the possibility that the weaker the resistance to tax hikes, the higher the tax morale; if people have high tax morale, they pay taxes regardless of government coercion. Conversely, the larger the resistance to tax hikes, the lower the tax morale.

In light of the Japanese response to the consumption tax hike, it may be assumed that Japanese taxpayers have a high level of tax resistance and a low tax morale. However, the reality is that tax morale is often regarded as high in Japan. For example, Tekeli's (2011) research with the World Value Survey (hear after the WVS) found that Japan has the highest degree of tax morale. Contrary to the results of the surveys conducted by the Japanese media and the setbacks the Japanese government has faced over the past several national elections, Japanese people are inclined to pay taxes regardless of a sense of duty.

In response to the aforementioned contradictory facts, we designed our survey in step with the following objectives. First, we sought to confirm whether tax morale

T. Miyazaki et al., *Tax Morale and Tax Resistance*, Kobe University Social Science Research Series, https://doi.org/10.1007/978-981-19-0478-3_3

among Japanese taxpayers was high. For comparison, we used the same questions as the WVS. Second, we tried to highlight tax resistance. In particular, based on the fact that taxpayers in Japan seem to have a psychological resistance to consumption tax hikes, we focused on consumption tax. Since the Japanese government increased the consumption tax rate in October 2019, we capitalized this event and asked respondents their opinions on consumption tax before and after the tax hike. Further, we also examined attitudes toward fiscal adjustment and the people's tax burden in the follow-up survey.

We delegated the survey to the Rakuten Insight Company. We implemented the survey twice. Both were conducted online. The first survey was conducted from August 26 to 28, 2019. There were 7000 respondents, and Japanese citizens over the age of 15 were randomly chosen. We also conducted a second survey from July 7 to 9, 2020. Following the company's guidelines for follow-up surveys, the second survey sample comprised 3750 respondents. To construct panel data for estimation, we ensured that the respondents of the follow-up survey had also completed the first survey.

Appendices 1 and 2 present the questionnaires of the first and second surveys.

3.2 Outline of the First Survey

Question 1 is as follows.

Please answer this question if you were in such a situation.

Please tell me for each of the following statements whether you think it can always be justified, never justified, or something in between: (...) cheating on tax if you have the chance.

("never justified"—code 1 from a ten-point scale where 1 = never and 10 = always).

We replicated this question on tax morale from the WVS. One concern was that some respondents, especially younger ones who do not pay tax, may not answer this question. To avoid this, we designed our survey as follows. First, the respondents could not proceed to the next question until they completed the current question (e.g., the respondent must answer Question 1 to move on to Question 2). This was also the case in the second survey. Second, we did not offer a "no answer" option. Third, we designed Questions 2, 3, and 8 to examine the respondent's sensitivity to tax information to clarify each respondent's tax compliance level.

In conjunction, Questions 10 to 13 asked respondents about their attitudes regarding the government's credibility, the political party they supported, and their senses of right and wrong, in step with the WVS.

Regarding the consumption tax hike, we first sought opinions on the October 2019 tax increase via Question 4. Question 5 was set such that respondents could indicate their ideal consumption tax rate. That is why some respondents might have felt that their tax burden was so high that they preferred a lower consumption tax rate; others might have felt that a higher consumption tax rate was acceptable because they would reap substantial benefit from public services in exchange for the higher tax burden.

We also asked opinions on measures to mitigate business fluctuation and the reduced tax system via Questions 6 and 7.

We then asked about the effects of debt accumulation on consumption (Question 9) and economic literacy (Questions 14 to 17) based upon Hayo et al.'s (2014) representative survey in Germany. Questions 18 to 21 asked respondents about their risk and time preferences by replicating the questionnaire by the Institute of Social and Economic Research of Osaka University (hereafter OU panel). We also used the OU panel questions to design Questions 25 to 35, which focused on income, asset, and debt levels and whether respondents lived with their families.

Questions 22 to 24 asked about the current and future prospects of each respondent's economic status, following Hayo et al. (2014), the OU panel, and the Japan General Social Survey (JGSS). We also used questions from these three surveys to collect respondents' education and job information in Questions 36 through 38.

3.3 Outline of the Second Survey

The follow-up survey had two objectives. First, we sought to check the difference regarding some items before and after the consumption tax hike in 2019. Second, we confirmed attitudes toward fiscal adjustment, approval of universal basic income (hereafter UBI), the tax burden, and coronavirus relief.

As noted earlier, the Japanese government has being running a deficit since the early 1990s; accordingly, Japan's debt-to-GDP ratio is the highest among some developed countries. While these are well known facts among economists, non-experts are not familiar with the exact size of Japan's government debt or deficit. As mentioned in Roth et al. (2021), knowledge about the government deficit may affect preferences for lowering the national debt and attitudes towards government expenditures and, along these lines, attitudes towards tax policy, including tax compliance and pandemic measures. To address these issues, we divided the respondents into two groups and compared how their understandings of the financial condition of the government affected their attitudes toward fiscal consolidation, tax morale, and coronavirus relief.

Group 1 was first shown the below question.

GDP measures a society's total income and its total expenditure on newly produced goods and services.[1] Meanwhile, there is an indicator called "the long-term debt outstanding" of central and local governments (hereafter, long-term government debt). To capture the financial conditions, we often use the $\frac{\text{long-term government debt}}{GDP}$ by considering the two indicators.

At the end of Fiscal Year (hearafter FY) 1998, the $\frac{\text{long-term government debt}}{GDP}$ in Japan was 105%. This means that the Japanese government owed a little bit more than the country produced in that year.

How large do you think the $\frac{\text{long-term government debt}}{GDP}$ was at the end of FY 2018? Please input your response in the space below.

[1] The definition of GDP follows Mankiw (2019).

			%

After this question, the respondent was expected to move on to the next and subsequent questions, as shown in Appendix 2.

Group 2 was first asked Questions 5 to 16 before being given questions on the size of the public debt and their opinions toward fiscal adjustment (Questions 1 to 4 of Appendix 2). Thus, this process allowed us to compare the response between the two groups regarding tax morale (Question 5), opinion on tax liability (Questions 6 and 7), "ideal" consumption tax rate (Question 8), opinion on the reduced tax rate (Question 9), opinion on coronavirus relief (Questions 10 and 11), and opinion on the introduction of UBI (Questions 12 to 16).

Questions 2 and 3 followed the work of Roth et al. (2021) and Question 4 was based on Hayo et al. (2014). We constructed the questions regarding UBI following previous studies such as Hayo et al. (2014) and Stadelmann-Steffen and Dermont (2020). UBI is a government-guaranteed payment that each citizen receives every month, regardless of income, wealth, and job status. The government provides sufficient coverage of the basic cost of living through this program. We also introduced the questions on UBI because some people advocate that UBI should be introduced by reducing some taxes.[2] Questions 15 and 16 were designed to consider UBI in light of the fact that unemployment will increase due to the progress of Artificial Intelligence (AI) and the automation of production, as indicated by Acemoglu and Restrepo (2018).

Questions 17 to 19 sought to gather knowledge on tax policy and the sources of this knowledge.

We also asked the same questions as the first survey. For example, we set Questions 5, 20, 21, and 22 to check the difference in tax morale and its foundation before and after the consumption tax hike. We also confirmed any change in the respondent's "ideal" tax rate (Question 8) and in their opinion of the reduced tax rate system (Question 9). Questions 23 and above were the same as those in the first survey. They were set to compare the change in the respondent's economic outlook (Questions 23 and 24), income and assets (Questions 25 to 28), and health and job (Questions 29 and 30).

3.4 Limiting Respondents and Checking Representativeness

We first tested the stated numbers from different surveys. To do this, we compared our results with those of the WVS. In particular, we focused on results related to tax morale (Question 1 in the first survey and Question 5 in the follow-up survey) because they enabled us to compare our surveys with the WVS. Additionally, the

[2] As an example, in Japan, please also see the article:
https://asia.nikkei.com/Politics/Japan-party-calls-for-Andrew-Yang-style-universal-basic-income.

survey on Japan was conducted in September 2019 during the WVS Wave 7 (2017–2020), around the time of our first survey; this timing makes the two surveys rather comparable. Although we limited the sample period for the reason discussed in the next page, we first compared the original data from the 7500 respondents of our first survey with the data from the WVS. In total, 45.8% of the 7500 respondents chose "never justified" in response to Question 1; the corresponding fraction for the WVS was 86.5%. We tested whether these two ratios were statistically different and found that they were even at a 1% significance level.

In the meantime, the respondents' personal information was kept private during both surveys. Our survey was conducted via the Internet, while mailing methods are usually used in the WVS; however, in both surveys, we have to pay attention to the fact that respondents do not answer questions in the presence of the interviewer. Notably, people without regular access to the Internet and/or people who are unfamiliar with the Internet—typically old people—were practically excluded from our survey; this is not the case with the WVS since it uses the mail. This difference may explain the difference in the age profiles of the two surveys: the average age of our 2019 survey was 48.5 years, while that of the WVS was 54.7 years old; this difference is statistically different at the 1% significance level. In our first survey, the correlation coefficient between age and answers for Q1 (from 1 to 10) was −0.013026, and was statistically different from zero even at the 1% significance level. Since our surveys were conducted by the Internet, younger people were more represented. We suspect that this may be why fewer respondents chose "never justified" in our survey than in the WVS.[3]

When we conducted the first survey, we asked respondents about (1) whether they delegated their tax declaration to a tax accountant (Question 8), (2) the values of their salary and assets (Questions 25 to 31), and (3) whether they were labor union members (Question 37). We created "no response" and "unknown/unsure" options for Questions 8. We cannot rule out the possibility that respondents intentionally chose one of these response options because they refused to answer. Because this may have also been the case for Questions 26 and 27 in the first survey and Question 26 in the follow-up survey, we omitted respondents who answered "no response" and "unknown/unsure" to Questions 8, 26, and 27 on the first survey and Question 26 in the second survey; this reduced our sample size to 2,109.

Next, we checked the representativeness of the survey. We compared the latest national census, which was conducted in 2015, with our survey. As stated earlier, the online format of our questionnaire caused younger people to be more represented than elderly people among respondents. In fact, as shown in Fig. 3.1, respondents aged 30–49 years comprised half the sample of our first survey. This does not align with the age distribution reported in the 2015 national census. Furthermore, Figs. 3.2a and b show that while men comprise 48.2% of 2005 national census population, they comprise 58.9% of our 2019 sample. Furthermore, as Figs. 3.3a and b reveal, the correspondence level was high for residential areas and household structure in the

[3] The average age of the reduced sample for our first survey is 51.3 years old. The difference between this and 54.7 in WVS is also found to be statistically different from zero at the 1% level.

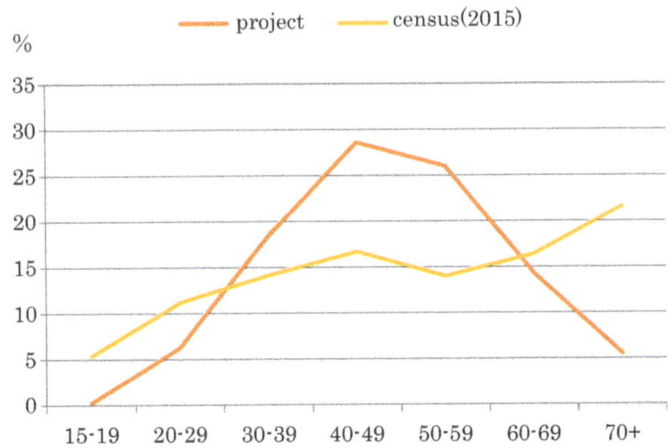

Fig. 3.1 Age distribution between our survey and the national census (The number of the respondents = 7500)

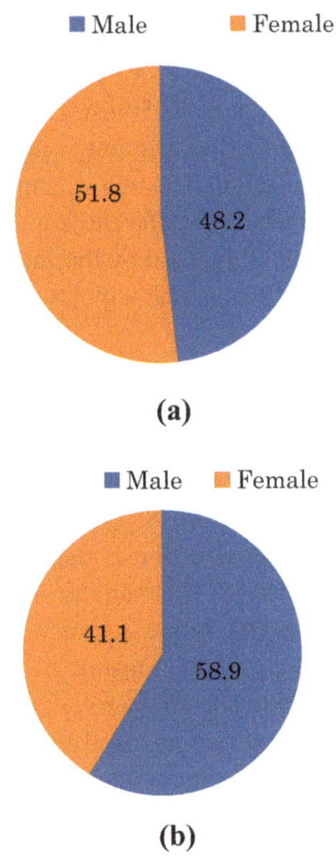

Fig. 3.2 **a** Proportions of male and female respondents (the national census), **b** proportions of male and female respondents (our first survey). (The number of the respondents = 7500)

first survey. Moreover, Figs. 3.4a and b show that even when we limit the sample to 2109, the distribution of residential areas and household structure is almost identical to that in Figs. 3.3a and b; this confirms the representativeness of residential areas and household structure.

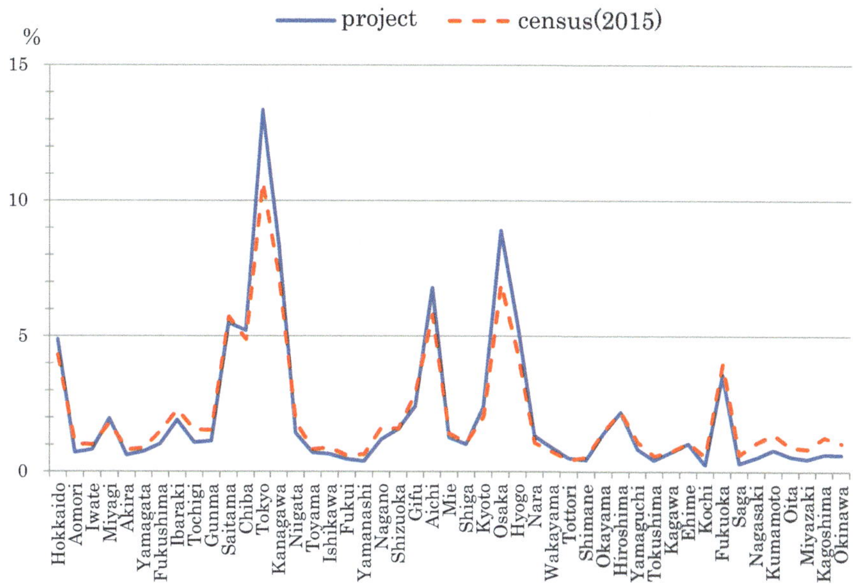

(a)

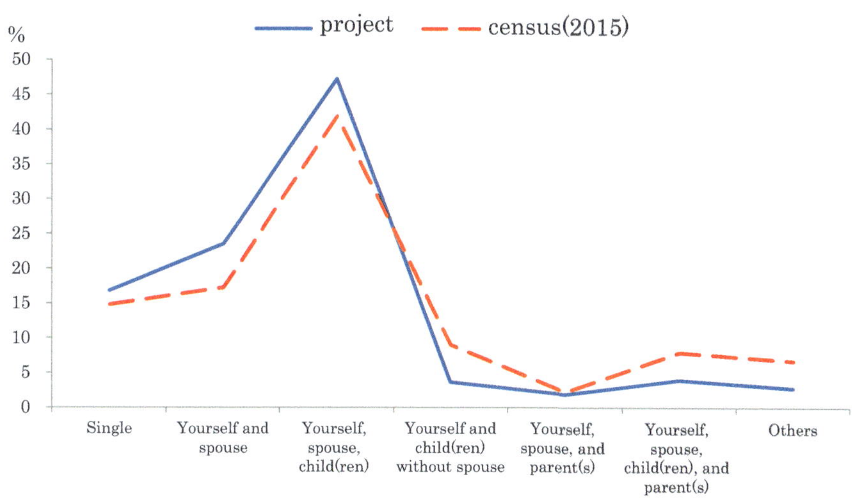

(b)

Fig. 3.3 **a** Regional distribution between our survey and the national census (the number of the respondents = 7500), **b** household structure between our survey and the national census (the number of the respondents = 7500)

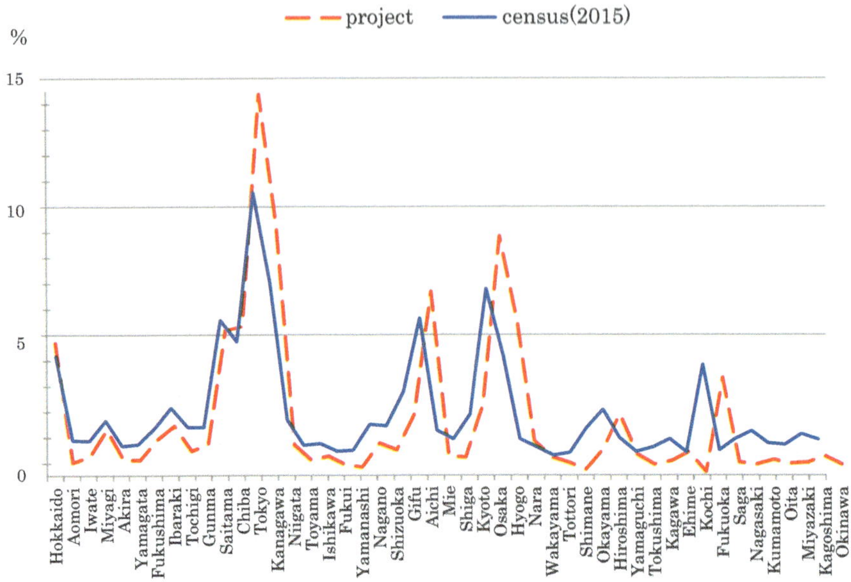

(a)

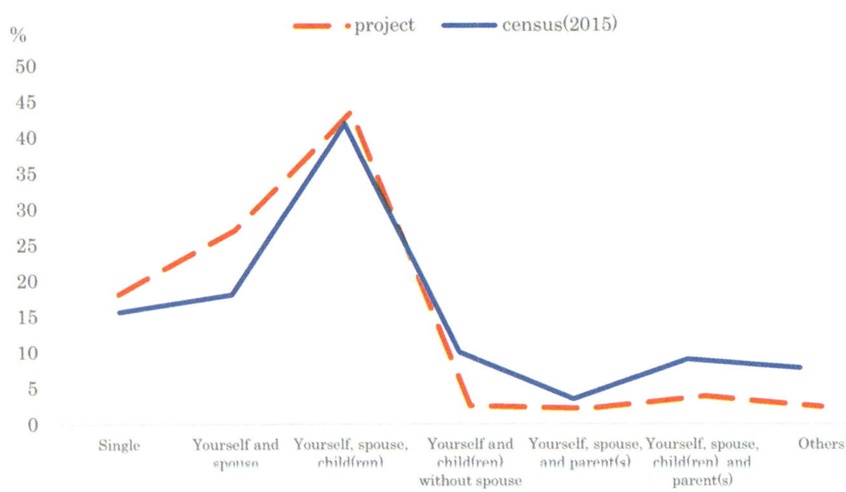

(b)

Fig. 3.4 **a** Regional distribution between our survey and the national census (the number of the respondents=2109), **b** household structure between our survey and the national census (the number of the respondents=2109)

Appendix

We further compared our results with the WVS to bolster the arguments of Sect. 3.4. First, we compared the reduced sample of our 2019 survey (2109 observations) and the WVS. As reported in Table 4.1 (shown in Chap. 4) and as stated above, 45.8% of the sample chose "never justified" in the former and 86.5% in the latter; again, the difference was statistically different even at the 1% significance level.

Second, regarding our follow-up survey, we reduced the sample size from the full 3750 to 2109. The proportion of respondents who answered "never justified" reported in Table 4.2 (which is also shown in Chap. 4), 45.3%, was obtained from this reduced sample; this ratio was not statistically different from the 46% reported in Table 4.1 even at the conventional significance levels.

Finally, we conducted the same test between (i) the full samples of our first survey (7500 observations) and second survey (3750 observations), as well as (ii) between the common reduced samples of the two surveys (2109 observations for both surveys). In (i), the ratios of choosing "never justified" were 45.8% in the first survey (as stated above) and 45.45% in the second survey; the difference was *not* statistically different from zero at conventional significance levels. In (ii), the ratios of choosing "never justified" were 45.47% in the first survey (as stated above) and 45.45% in the second survey (as stated above); the difference was *not* statistically different from zero here as well.

References

Acemoglu D, Restrepo P (2018) Artificial intelligence, automation and work. NBER working Paper No. 24196

Hayo B, Neumeier, F, Matthias U (2014) Topics in fiscal policy: evidence from a representative survey of the German survey. MAGKS Discussion Paper No. 12–2014

Mankiw NG (2019) Macroeconomics, 10th edn. Macmillan

Luttmer EFP, Singhal M (2014) Tax morale. J Econ Perspect 28(4):149–168

Roth C, Settele S, Wohlfart J (2021) Beliefs about public debt and the demand for government spending. J Econometrics, Forthcoming

Stadelmann-Steffen I, Dermont C (2020) Citizens' opinions about basic income proposals compared: a conjoint analysis of Finland and Switzerland. J Soc Policy 49(2):383–403

Schmölders G (1965) Finanzpolitik, Zwite Auflage, Springer-Verlag

Tamaoka T (1994) The regressiveness of a value added tax: tax credit method and subtraction method: a Japanese case. Fiscal Stud 15(2):57–73

Tekeli R (2011) Determinants of tax morale in Japan and in Turkey. https://www.mof.go.jp/pri/international_exchange/visiting_scholar_program/ws2011_d.pdf

Chapter 4
Summary Statistics

Here we present summary statistics by focusing on the responses for tax morale and consumption tax hikes to demonstrate our objectives. Our summary statistics followed the work of Hayo et al. (2014).

4.1 Tax Morale and Tax Compliance

The first survey (Table 4.1) found that 45.5% of respondents believed that cheating on taxes is never justifiable. In total, more than 60% of respondents considered underreporting or concealing their income to be unfavorable. Regarding the follow-up survey (Table 4.2), 45.3% of the respondents chose "1," similar to the first survey.

Meanwhile, several notable events took place between the two surveys, including the consumption tax hike, political scandals, and the coronavirus pandemic. The political scandals included the prime minister being suspected of making an illegal donation to his constituents and the arrest of the former justice minister. Accordingly, the approval rating for the cabinet collected by the NHK, the national broadcasting corporation, decreased from 45% in July 2019 to 34% in August 2020.[1] Overall, political scandals increased political mistrust. Moreover, many people felt the government's coronavirus policy response was insufficient. However, as Tables 4.1 and 4.2 suggest, respondent answers to the tax morale question did not significantly change between the two surveys; in this sense, these government blunders did not affect taxpayers' nonpecuniary motivation.

[1] Please see the below website: https://bainesreport.org/2020/11/what-will-and-will-not-change-in-japan-part-1/.

T. Miyazaki et al., *Tax Morale and Tax Resistance*, Kobe University Social Science Research Series, https://doi.org/10.1007/978-981-19-0478-3_4

Table 4.1 Summary statistics for tax morale (Question 1 of the first survey)

	Proportion	S.E.	C.I.		Count
			Low	Upper	
1 Never justified	0.455	0.021	0.433	0.476	959
2	0.097	0.013	0.084	0.109	204
3	0.108	0.013	0.094	0.121	227
4	0.040	0.008	0.032	0.049	85
5	0.164	0.016	0.148	0.180	346
6	0.052	0.009	0.042	0.061	109
7	0.037	0.008	0.029	0.045	78
8	0.018	0.006	0.012	0.024	38
9	0.009	0.004	0.005	0.014	20
10 Always justified	0.020	0.006	0.014	0.026	43
Total	1.000				2109

Table 4.2 Summary statistics for tax morale (Question 5 of the second survey)

	Proportion	S.E.	C.I.		Count
			Low	Upper	
1 Never justified	0.453	0.021	0.432	0.474	955
2	0.098	0.013	0.085	0.111	207
3	0.115	0.014	0.101	0.128	242
4	0.052	0.009	0.042	0.061	109
5	0.168	0.016	0.152	0.184	355
6	0.045	0.009	0.036	0.053	94
7	0.032	0.007	0.024	0.039	67
8	0.019	0.006	0.013	0.025	40
9	0.004	0.003	0.001	0.006	8
10 Always justfied	0.015	0.005	0.010	0.020	32
Total	1.000				2109

Furthermore, the summary statistics regarding public sector and politician trust did not substantially change between the two surveys (Figs. 4.1, 4.2 and 4.3). Although the proportion of respondents who answered "mistrust" in response to questions about politicians and the Diet increased by about four percentage points, political mistrust or trust did not change despite the scandals.

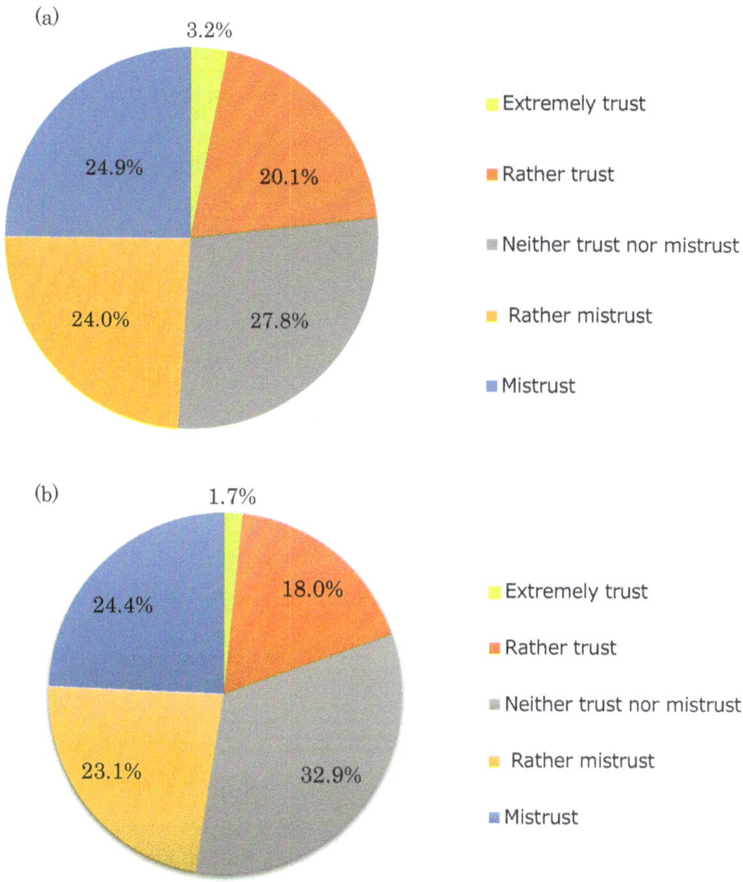

Fig. 4.1 **a** Trust regarding the central administrative office (Question 10 of the first survey). **b** Trust regarding the central administrative office (Question 20 of the second survey)

When it comes to some questions on tax compliance (Table 4.3), about 45% of the respondents paid no attention to tax policy information. Thus, taxpayers in Japan are not necessarily eager to collect information on tax policies. However, Table 4.4 indicates that about 70% of respondents properly pay their taxes. Recall that Japanese taxpayers have a high level of tax morale according to the WVS and our two surveys; this can be attributed to the fact that they tend to abide by the rules.

We also ascertained taxpayers' sense of burden related to their tax payments. Tables 4.5 and 4.6 reveal that more than 60% of respondents more or less felt burdened by high income taxes, regardless of their awareness of the size of government debt. Regarding the consumption tax burden, Table 4.7 shows that given information on the real outstanding government debt, about 55% of the respondents think their consumption tax burden is high or a little high and Table 4.8 shows that 68% of respondents feel this way without information on government debt. These results

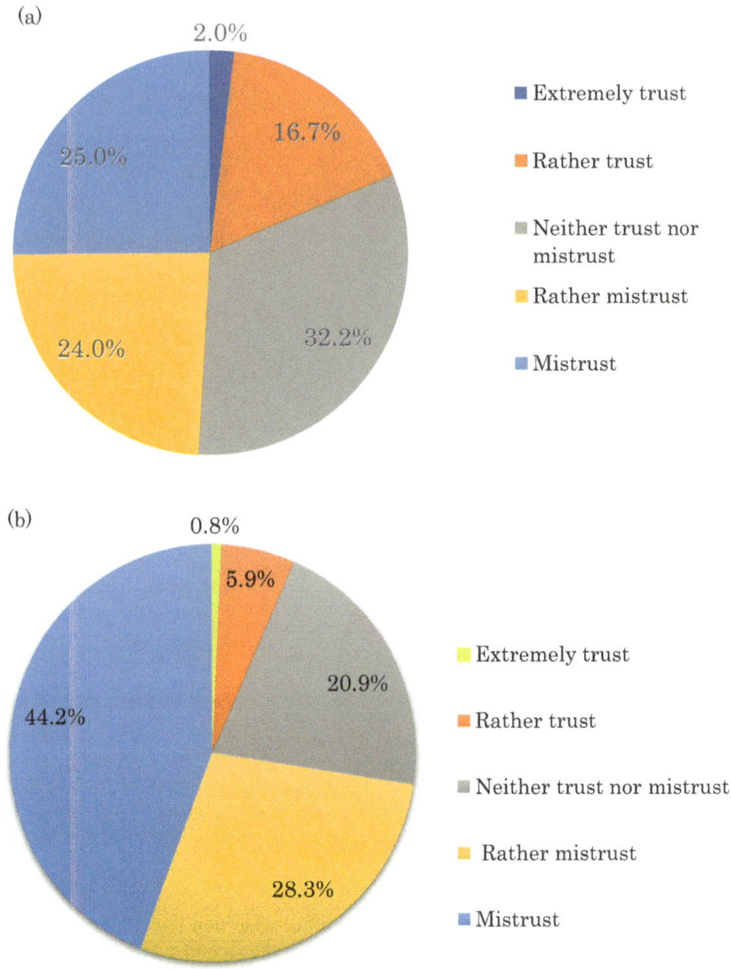

Fig. 4.2 **a** Trust regarding National Diet members (Question 10 of the first survey). **b** Trust regarding National Diet members (Question 20 of the second survey)

imply that a taxpayer's sense of the degree to which consumption tax is a burden may change in accordance with their information on the size of Japan's government debt; indeed, the difference between the two groups is statistically significant. We thus confirmed that government budget information generates this difference among correspondents.

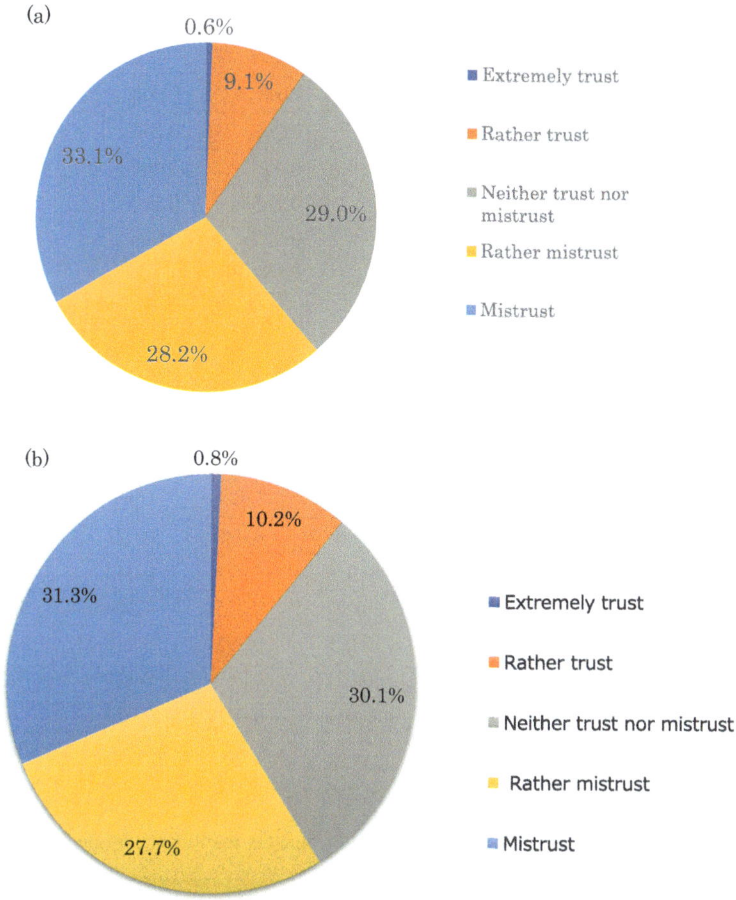

Fig. 4.3 **a** Trust regarding local assembly members (Question 10 of the first survey). **b** Trust regarding local assembly members (Question 20 of the second survey)

Table 4.3 Summary statistics for the question on whether a respondent gathers information on tax (Question 2 of the first survey)

	Proportion	S.E.	C.I.		Count
			Low	Upper	
1 Always	0.038	0.008	0.030	0.046	80
2	0.225	0.018	0.207	0.243	475
3	0.281	0.019	0.262	0.300	592
4	0.263	0.019	0.244	0.281	554
5 Never	0.193	0.017	0.177	0.210	408
Total	1.000				2109

Table 4.4 Summary statistics for attention given to tax payment (Question 3 of the first survey)

	Proportion	S.E.	C.I.		Count
			Low	Upper	
1 Very careful	0.226	0.018	0.208	0.244	477
2	0.446	0.021	0.425	0.467	941
3	0.182	0.016	0.165	0.198	383
4	0.084	0.012	0.072	0.096	177
5 Little careful	0.062	0.010	0.052	0.072	131
Total	1.000				2109

Table 4.5 Summary statistics for the question on income tax liability (Question 6 of the second survey, Group 1)

	Proportion	S.E.	C.I.		Count
			Low	Upper	
Low	0.015	0.007	0.008	0.022	16
Slightly low	0.031	0.010	0.021	0.042	34
Appropriate	0.282	0.027	0.255	0.308	307
Slightly higher	0.318	0.028	0.291	0.346	347
High	0.296	0.027	0.269	0.323	323
Not paying income tax	0.058	0.014	0.044	0.072	63
Total	1.000				1090

Table 4.6 Summary statistics for the question on income tax liability (Question 6 of the second survey, Group 2)

	Proportion	S.E.	C.I.		Count
			Low	Upper	
Low	0.015	0.007	0.007	0.022	15
Slightly low	0.028	0.010	0.018	0.039	29
Appropriate	0.184	0.024	0.161	0.208	188
Slightly higher	0.313	0.028	0.285	0.342	319
High	0.392	0.030	0.362	0.422	399
Not paying income tax	0.068	0.015	0.052	0.083	69
Total	1.000				1019

4.2 Tax Resistance

In the first survey, almost half of the respondents were against the tax hike (Table 4.9). Further, more than 60% of them reported that their "ideal" consumption tax rate ranged between 0 and 9% (Fig. 4.4). Regarding measures to mitigate business cycle fluctuations (Table 4.10), 46% of respondents were against measures such as the

Table 4.7 Summary statistics for the question on consumption tax burden (Question 7 of the second survey, Group 1)

	Proportion	S.E.	C.I.		Count
			Low	Upper	
Low	0.019	0.008	0.011	0.027	21
Slightly low	0.094	0.017	0.076	0.111	102
Appropriate	0.340	0.028	0.312	0.368	371
Slightly higher	0.312	0.028	0.284	0.339	340
High	0.235	0.025	0.210	0.260	256
Total	1.000				1090

Table 4.8 Summary statistics for the question on consumption tax burden (Question 7 of the second survey, Group 2)

	Proportion	S.E.	C.I.		Count
			Low	Upper	
Low	0.011	0.006	0.004	0.017	11
Slightly low	0.039	0.012	0.027	0.051	40
Appropriate	0.270	0.027	0.243	0.297	275
Slightly higher	0.326	0.029	0.297	0.355	332
High	0.354	0.029	0.325	0.384	361
Total	1.000				1019

Table 4.9 Summary statistics for the attitude toward the October 2019 consumption tax hike (Question 4 of the first survey)

	Proportion	S.E.	C.I.		Count
			Low	Upper	
Disagree	0.298	0.020	0.278	0.317	628
Disagree a little	0.226	0.018	0.208	0.244	476
Neither agree nor disagree	0.210	0.017	0.192	0.227	442
Agree a little	0.224	0.018	0.206	0.242	473
Strongly agree	0.043	0.009	0.034	0.051	90
Total	1.000				2109

premium gift certificates or the rebate. Respondents may feel that these measures are not necessarily useful for mitigating business cycles, even if an economic stimulus package is needed to curve the economic downturn caused by a tax hike. When it comes to the reduced tax system, the pros and cons were divided as shown in Table 4.11. The reduced tax rate system was criticized by many economists in Japan,

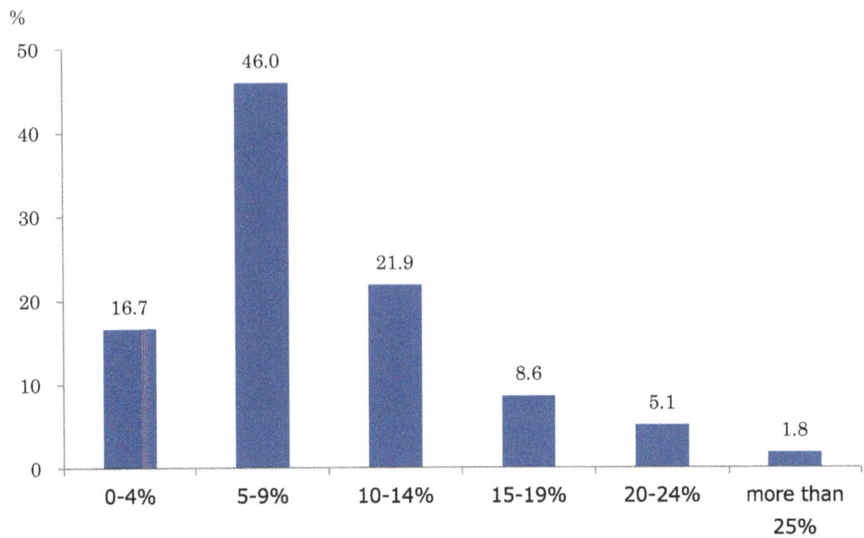

Fig. 4.4 Distribution of the "ideal" consumption tax rate (The results for Question 5 of the first survey)

Table 4.10 Summary statistics for the opinion on measures to reduce the burden of tax increases (Question 6 of the first survey)

	Proportion	S.E.	C.I.		Count
			Low	Upper	
Disagree	0.259	0.019	0.240	0.278	546
Disagree a little	0.205	0.017	0.188	0.223	433
Neither agree nor disagree	0.232	0.018	0.214	0.250	490
Agree a little	0.235	0.018	0.217	0.253	496
Strongly agree	0.068	0.011	0.058	0.079	144
Total	1.000				2109

Table 4.11 Summary statistics for the opinion on reduced tax rate (Question 7 of the first survey)

	Proportion	S.E.	C.I.		Count
			Low	Upper	
Disagree	0.201	0.017	0.183	0.218	423
Disagree a little	0.152	0.015	0.137	0.168	321
Neither agree nor disagree	0.193	0.017	0.176	0.210	407
Agree a little	0.302	0.020	0.282	0.322	637
Strongly agree	0.152	0.015	0.137	0.168	321
Total	1.000				2109

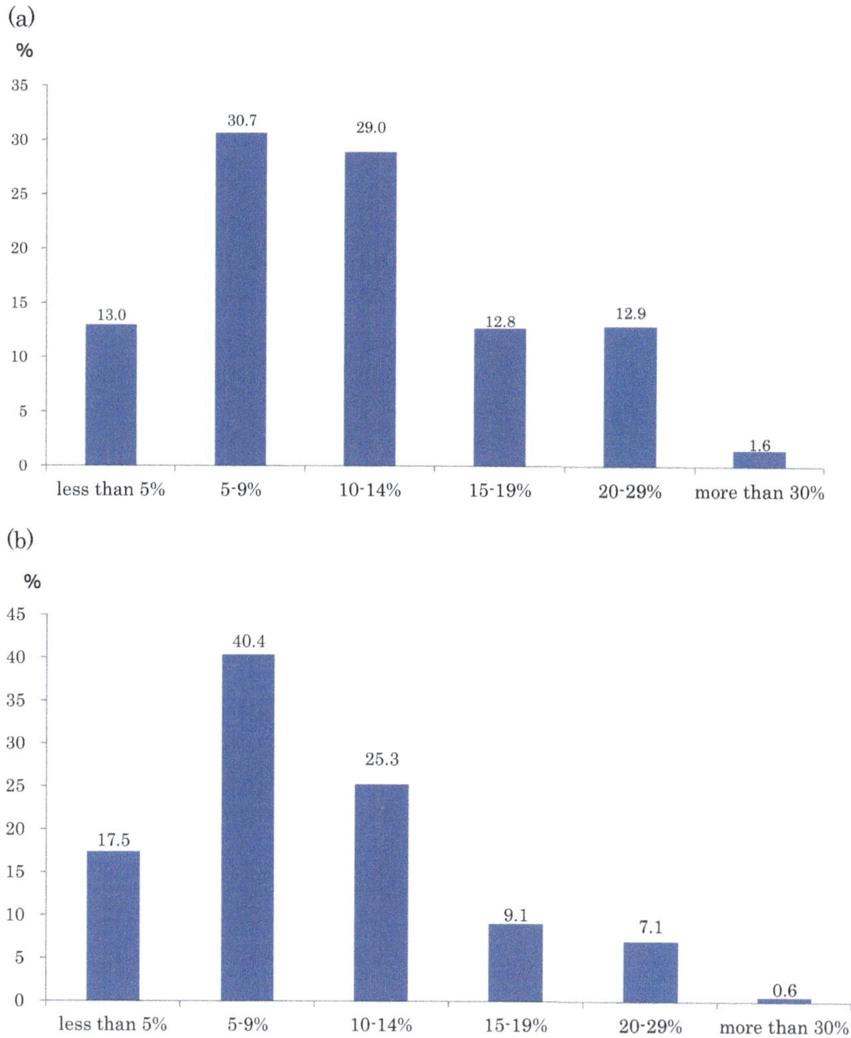

Fig. 4.5 **a** Distribution of the "ideal" consumption tax rate (The results for Question 8 of the second survey, Group 1). **b** Distribution of the "ideal" consumption tax rate (The results for Question 8 of the second survey, Group 2)

while media and the ruling parties pushed its introduction.[2] Since the respondents may have been affected by both opinions, we could not show decisive results.

In the follow-up survey (Fig. 4.5), the result for Group 1 revealed that more than half of the respondents think their ideal consumption tax rate should be over 10%.

---

[2] Regarding criticism on the reduced tax rate, please see the below website: https://www.nira.or.jp/pdf/e_vision26.pdf.

However, about 60% of respondents without information on the size of the government debt felt the consumption tax rate should be less than 10% (Fig. 4.5). Figure 4.5 also shows that approximately 30% of respondents suppose the consumption tax rate to be more than 15% with respect to Group 1, whose fraction was larger than that of Group 2.

4.3 Observation from the Correlation Matrix

Table 4.12 reports the correlation matrix for the relevant questions on the first survey. The table shows that while the relationship between tax morale or tax compliance and the indicators related to politicians and the government is insignificant, there is a slightly positive relationship between tax morale and the social norm or a sense of right and wrong. It implies that the source of high tax morale among the Japanese people can partly be explained by their motivation to abide by the rules or social norms. As stated earlier, Questions 13A to 13C were used as latent variables to measure social norms. However, to dig deeper into the source of high tax morale, we have to conduct econometric investigations. Furthermore, since tax morale seems to be affected by some of the factors that give rise to opinions on policy, we could use some of our survey results on economic policy as independent variables during

Table 4.12 Correlation matrix for the first survey

		Q1	Q2	Q3	Q4	Q5	Q6	Q7
		Tax morale	Interest in tax policy	Filing tax properly	Opinion for consumption tax hike	"Ideal" consumption tax rate	Opinion for the measures	Opinion for the dual-system
Q10A	Trust: Central government	0.1031	0.0499	0.0426	-0.304	-0.2185	-0.1736	-0.0563
Q10B	Trust: National diet	0.0635	0.0635	0.0123	-0.2376	-0.1729	-0.2	-0.073
Q10C	Trust: Local assembly	0.0786	0.0769	0.0567	-0.1957	-0.1232	-0.1828	-0.0942
Q11A	Influence on politics	-0.0967	-0.1096	-0.0897	0.0624	0.0519	-0.0136	-0.0301
Q11B	Understanding of politics	-0.0756	-0.1658	-0.1251	0.1221	0.1102	-0.0633	-0.076
Q11C	Influence of our vote	-0.1492	-0.0869	-0.1544	0.0692	0.0463	-0.0767	-0.0309
Q11D	The attitude of politicians	-0.0314	-0.042	0.0023	0.1661	0.15	0.1099	0.0036
Q13A	Cheating government benefits	0.2716	-0.0456	0.0956	-0.0384	0.008	0.0622	0.0044
Q13B	Avoiding a transportation fare	0.2187	0.0043	0.1606	-0.0358	0.0166	0.034	0.0072
Q13C	On stealing	0.2366	-0.0261	0.1487	-0.0195	0.0275	0.0357	-0.0021

Note For the details of each question, please see Appendix A

econometric exercises. Furthermore, it is necessary to address the psychological factors behind tax morale.

Regarding tax resistance, there is a slightly negative relationship between Questions 4, 10A, and 10B. This implies that political distrust may cultivate resistance to further tax hikes, as indicated by Scholz and Lubell (1988), Lacy (1998), and Yamamura (2014).

References

Hayo B, Neumeier F, Matthias U (2014) Topics in fiscal policy: evidence from a representative survey of the German survey. MAGKS discussion paper No. 12-2014

Lacy D (1998) Electoral support for tax cuts: a case study of the 1980 American presidential election. Am Polit Q 26(3):288–307

Scholz JT, Lubell M (1988) Trust and taxpaying: testing the heuristic approach to collective action. Am J Polit Sci 42(2):398–417

Yamamura E (2014) Trust in government and its effect on preferences for income redistribution and perceived tax burden. Econ Gov 15(1):71–100

Chapter 5
Conclusion

This book provides background information and basic descriptive statistics from the Internet survey on tax and fiscal policies in Japan. While Japanese taxpayers have high levels of tax morale and tax compliance, they do not necessarily approve of the October 2019 consumption tax hike. Furthermore, many taxpayers believe the consumption tax rate should be below 10%.

While Japanese taxpayers have high tax morale, they are also very resistant to consumption tax hikes; our correlation matrix suggests this may be due to their distrust of politicians and the government. Meanwhile, business owners may be afraid of bearing the tax burden through declines in their sales.[1] To confirm this, we compared respondents who were and were not self-employed using Question 4 in the first survey. We did this with our original sample, which yielded 7500 observations, as reported in Sect. 3.4. We found that 39.3% of these respondents were self-employed and 31.1% were not self-employed; these findings were statistically different. Among the self-employed, 63.0% chose "disagree" or "disagree a little"; among those who were not self-employed, 56.5% chose these options. These results were also statistically different. The ratios are smaller for the group that was not self-employed; this suggests that this group is less resistant than the self-employed group to the tax hike.

However, more econometric analyses are required to delve into the factors behind the results. This study concentrates on providing background information and details on the survey and summary statistics, and more empirical exercises are required in our future work. When it comes to tax morale, we cannot rule out the possibility that peoples' attitudes may vary according to the type of taxes they are asked to consider. Since we replicated the WVS and compared our results with its own, we only followed the WVS in examining tax morale. It would be worthwhile to investigate tax morale and tax compliance for different taxes in future surveys.

---

[1] Indeed, Homma (1992) points out that small traders feared that they would have to bear a consumption tax burden when the introduction of consumption tax was discussed in the 1980s in Japan.

T. Miyazaki et al., *Tax Morale and Tax Resistance*, Kobe University Social Science Research Series, https://doi.org/10.1007/978-981-19-0478-3_5

Reference

Homma M (1992) Tax reform in Japan. In: Ito T, Krueger AO (eds) The political economy of tax reform. University of Chicago Press, pp 65–95

Appendix A
Each Item of the First Survey

This questionnaire aims to survey opinions on Japan's tax policy and the financial conditions of the Japanese government. We would appreciate it if you answer all the questions, though you may feel some of them are a little bit technical.

We will use these results solely for academic research. Furthermore, since all the results are anonymous, your personal information will be kept confidential.

Thank you very much for your cooperation.

1. [Please answer this question if you were in such a situation.]
   Please tell me whether you think it can always be justified, never justified, or something in between: (…) Cheating on tax if you have the chance.
   ("never justified" – code 1 from a ten-point scale, where 1 = never and 10 = always).
2. Do you collect information on tax payments regularly through the media and tax office advertisements?
   ("always" – code 1 from a five-point scale, where 1 = always and 5 = never).
3. Are you careful in paying taxes by collecting information on taxes?
   ("Very careful" – code 1 from a five-point scale, where 1 = very careful and 5 = little careful).
4. Do you agree with the consumption tax increase scheduled in the fall of 2019?
   ("disagree" – code 1 from a five-point scale, where 1 = disagree and 5 = strongly agree).
5. Please tell us how high the consumption tax rate should be in Japan. Please write the specific numbers. Of course, "lower than 8%" is also acceptable.
6. In parallel with the consumption tax hike scheduled in October 2019, the Japanese government will offer premium gift certificates for households with children between 0 and 3 years old, low-income earners, and households with low public pensions for half a year. Moreover, if you make purchases with a credit card or electronic money, you will be awarded a maximum of 5 percent of the value of the purchases. Do you agree with these policies to reduce the burden of tax increases?
   ("disagree" – code 1 from a five-point scale, where 1 = disagree and 5 = strongly agree)

T. Miyazaki et al., *Tax Morale and Tax Resistance*, Kobe University Social Science Research Series, https://doi.org/10.1007/978-981-19-0478-3

7. While the consumption tax rate will be raised to 10% in October 2019, the rate will remain 8% for daily necessities. Do you agree with this policy? ("disagree" – code 1 from a five-point scale, where 1 = disagree and 5 = strongly agree)
8. Do you consult a tax accountant for professional advice when filing your taxes?
    1. All of the time
    2. Some of the time
    3. Never
    4. Not applicable (withholding income taxpayers)
    5. No response
9. We have seen an accelerated increase in public debt. The government will inevitably have to increase the tax rate or decrease expenditures, such as pensions and social security benefits. Did this situation lead to changes in your spending or saving behavior?

    Yes, I now spend a smaller proportion of my income and save a larger proportion.
    Yes, I spend a larger proportion of my income and save a smaller proportion.
    No, I did not change my behavior due to the rapid increase in public debt.

10. To what extent do you trust each of the following entities (A to C)? (1. Extremely trust, 2. Rather trust, 3. Neither trust nor mistrust, 4. Rather mistrust, 5. Mistrust)

A. Central administrative office	1	2	3	4	5
B. National Diet members	1	2	3	4	5
C. Local assembly members	1	2	3	4	5

11. How much do you agree with the following opinions from A to C? Please state your level of agreement on a scale of 1 (disagree) to 5 (agree).
    A. Civilians cannot influence a government.
    B. Government activities and politics are complicated; thus, people do not understand them.
    C. Your vote is too small to influence the election results because many people vote in the election.
    D. Roughly speaking, it seems that the National Diet members do not attempt to care for their constituents after their election win.
12. Please choose which of the following political parties you support.
    1. Liberal Democratic Party
    2. Constitutional Democratic Party of Japan
    3. Democratic Party for the People
    4. Japan Innovation Party
    5. Komeito

6. Japanese Communist Party
7. Social Democratic Party
8. Other political parties in Japan
9. Unaffiliated voters

13. [Please answer this question if you were in such a situation.]

    13A. Do you think the following statement can always be justified, never justified, or something in between? Please answer your opinion on a scale of 0 to 3 (3 = never and 0 = always).
    Receiving government benefits or subsidies for which one is not eligible.

    13B. Do you think the following statement can always be justified, never justified, or something in between? Please answer your opinion on a scale of 0 to 3 (3 = never and 0 = always).
    Avoiding a fare on public transportation.

    13C. Do you think the following statement can always be justified, never justified, or something in between? Please answer your opinion on a scale of 0 to 3 (3 = never and 0 = always).
    Buying something you knew was stolen.

14. What do you think total Japanese government debt (both central and local) was at the end of Fiscal Year 2018? Please choose the answer you believe is correct.

    1. JPY 1,100 trillion
    2. JPY 800 trillion
    3. JPY 900 trillion
    4. JPY 1,300 trillion
    5. Other numbers
    6. No response

15. The figure below compares the national burden rates—a percentage of tax and social security burden to national income—for five Western countries. Please choose one of the following five statements on the current burden rate in Japan that you believe is correct.

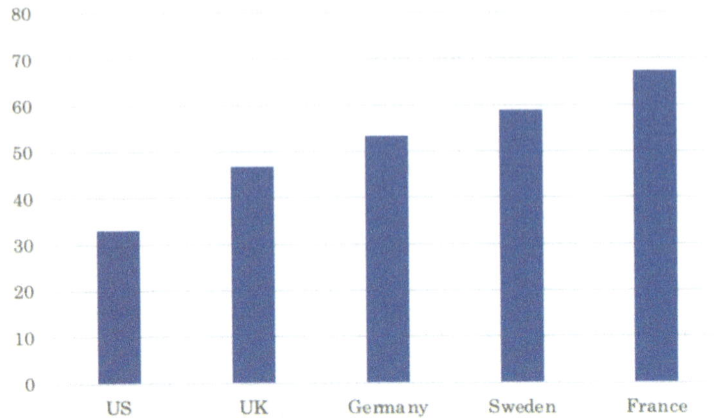

International comparison of national burden rates (2016). *Source* The website of the Ministry of Finance Japan

1. Japan's national burden rate is almost the same as that of the US at about 30%.
2. Japan's national burden rate is higher than that of the US but lower than that of the UK, between 40 and 50%.
3. Japan's national burden rate is almost the same as that of the UK, between 45 and 50%.
4. Japan's national burden rate is between 50 and 60%, similar to Germany and Sweden.
5. Japan's national burden rate is over 60%, like France.

16. By definition, long-term interest rates mean interest rates whose maturity is over one year. The most famous one is the 10-year government bond yield, which affects things like mortgage rates in financial markets. How much do you think the long-term interest rate is? Please choose the answer that you think is right.

    1. About −0.2%
    2. About 0%
    3. About 0.2%
    4. About 1.2%
    5. Other numbers
    6. No response

17. The consumer price index (CPI), which captures the average price of goods and services in one country, is used to judge deflation or inflation. How much is the CPI in Japan? Please choose the answer that you believe is correct.

    1. −0.6%
    2. 0.0%
    3. 0.6%
    4. 1.2%

5. Other numbers
6. No response

18. Suppose there is a 50% chance that you will lose JPY 100,000 within a day. However, if you pay an insurance premium, you can recoup the losses even if you fail. Please decide whether to pay the premium or not when its cost is as listed in the table below.
(Select "A" if you pay a premium, and "B" if not in each row).

Insurance premium (JPY)		
	You pay a premium	You do not pay a premium
1,000	A	B
5,000	A	B
10,000	A	B
15,000	A	B
20,000	A	B
30,000	A	B
40,000	A	B
45,000	A	B
50,000	A	B

19. Typically, for what probability of rain would you take an umbrella?

More than [| |] %

20. Suppose you can get some money either today or seven days from today. However, the amount differs according to each option, as listed in the following nine combinations. Which option, A or B listed below, do you like? Please choose your selection for all nine combinations.

Combination 1: (A) You get JPY 3,005 today.
(B) You get JPY 3,014 seven days from today.
Combination 2: (A) You get JPY 3,003 today.
(B) You get JPY 3,297 seven days from today.
Combination 3: (A) You get JPY 3,008 today.
(B) You get JPY 3,037 seven days from today.
Combination 4: (A) You get JPY 3,000 today.
(B) You get JPY 3,000 seven days from today.
Combination 5: (A) You get JPY 3,005 today.
(B) You get JPY 5,951 seven days from today.
Combination 6: (A) You get JPY 3,009 today.
(B) You get JPY 3,068 seven days from today.

Combination 7: (A) You get JPY 3,001 today.
(B) You get JPY 3,119 seven days from today.
Combination 8: (A) You get JPY 3,002 today.
(B) You get JPY 2,996 seven days from today.
Combination 9: (A) You get JPY 3,008 today.
(B) You get JPY 3,011 seven days from today.

21. Suppose you can get some money either 90 days or 97 days from today. However, the amount differs according to each option, as listed in the following nine combinations. Which option listed below, A or B, do you like? Please make a selection for all nine combinations.

Combination 1: (A) You get JPY 3,005 after 90 days.
(B) You get JPY 3,118 after 97 days.
Combination 2: (A) You get JPY 3,006 after 90 days.
(B) You get JPY 3,000 after 97 days.
Combination 3: (A) You get JPY 3,000 after 90 days.
(B) You get JPY 3,009 after 97 days.
Combination 4: (A) You get JPY 3,007 after 90 days.
(B) You get JPY 3,301 after 97 days.
Combination 5: (A) You get JPY 3,006 after 90 days.
(B) You get JPY 3,035 after 97 days.
Combination 6: (A) You get JPY 3,002 after 90 days.
(B) You get JPY 3,005 after 97 days.
Combination 7: (A) You get JPY 3,007 after 90 days.
(B) You get JPY 5,955 after 97 days.
Combination 8: (A) You get JPY 3,001 after 90 days.
(B) You get JPY 3,001 after 97 days.
Combination 9: (A) You get JPY 3,007 after 90 days.
(B) You get JPY 3,066 after 97 days.

22. What do you think of the amount of public pension you will receive after your retirement compared to those who are currently receiving the pension? Choose the one that applies from the list below.

1. Will be much better
2. Will be a little bit better
3. Will be the same
4. Will be a little bit worse
5. Will be much worse
6. Unknown/unsure
7. I am currently receiving a public pension

23. How much do you worry about your future life from a financial perspective? Choose the one that applies from the list below.

1. Strongly agree

2. Agree a little
3. Neither
4. Disagree a little
5. Strongly disagree
6. Unknown/unsure

24. Suppose the current Japanese society is divided into ten tiers. Which tier currently applies to you? Choose the one that applies from the list below:

1	2	3	4	5	6	7	8	9	10
Highest									Lowest

25. What was the sum of you and your partner's pre-tax income in 2018? Please choose the closest option as follows. If you obtained bonuses other than monthly salaries, please include them in the calculation. If you are a student, please consider the income from a part-time job, allowance from your parents, scholarship, and so forth. Please choose the most appropriate option in the following section.

1. None.
2. Less than 1 million yen.
3. 1 million yen or over, but less than 2 million yen.
4. 2 million yen or over, but less than 4 million yen.
5. 4 million yen or over, but less than 6 million yen.
6. 6 million yen or over, but less than 8 million yen.
7. 8 million yen or over, but less than 10 million yen.
8. 10 million yen or over, but less than 12 million yen.
9. 12 million yen or over, but less than 14 million yen.
10. 14 million yen or over, but less than 16 million yen.
11. 16 million yen or over, but less than 18 million yen.
12. 18 million yen or over, but less than 20 million yen.
13. 20 million yen or over, but less than 22 million yen.
14. Over 22 million yen.
15. Not applicable.

26. How much is your household's real estate worth? If you are a student, please consider that of your parent(s). Please choose the most appropriate option in the following section.

1. No property.
2. Less than 5 million yen.
3. 5 million yen or over, but less than 10 million yen.
4. 10 million yen or over, but less than 15 million yen.
5. 15 million yen or over, but less than 20 million yen.
6. 20 million yen or over, but less than 30 million yen.
7. 30 million yen or over, but less than 40 million yen.

8. 40 million yen or over, but less than 50 million yen.
9. 50 million yen or over, but less than 100 million yen.
10. Over 100 million yen.
11. Unknown/unsure.

27. What is the total value of your household's financial assets (e.g., bank deposits, stocks, and insurance)? If you are a student, please consider those your parents hold. Choose the one that applies from the list below.

    1. Less than 2.5 million yen.
    2. 2.5 million yen or over, but less than 5 million yen.
    3. 5 million yen or over, but less than 7.5 million yen.
    4. 7.5 million yen or over, but less than 10 million yen.
    5. 10 million yen or over, but less than 15 million yen.
    6. 15 million yen or over, but less than 20 million yen.
    7. 20 million yen or over, but less than 30 million yen.
    8. 30 million yen or over, but less than 50 million yen.
    9. 50 million yen or over, but less than 100 million yen.
    10. Over 100 million yen.
    11. Unknown/unsure.

28. Choose the kind of housing in which you are currently living.

    1. Your own house (including the one owned by your parents)
    2. Apartment rented from a private firm
    3. Apartment provided by your company or apartment for public servants
    4. Apartment rented from a public housing agency
    5. Others (Specify)

29. Do you have to pay off loans? Include all debts, such as home mortgages, car loans, and loans for education.

    Yes, I have to pay off mortgages. → Go to Question 30.
    No, I do not have to pay off any mortgages. → Go to Questions 32 and 33.

30. How much of your home mortgage do you still have to pay off? Choose the one that applies from the list below.

    1. No mortgage.
    2. Less than 2.5 million yen.
    3. 2.5 million yen or over, but less than 5 million yen.
    4. 5 million yen or over, but less than 7.5 million yen.
    5. 7.5 million yen or over, but less than 10 million yen.
    6. 10 million yen or over, but less than 15 million yen.
    7. 15 million yen or over, but less than 20 million yen.
    8. 20 million yen or over, but less than 30 million yen.
    9. Over 30 million yen.

31. Do you have loans other than home mortgages? If so, choose the outstanding amount that applies from the list below. Include all types of loans from which you have to pay interest accrued.

    1. No loans other than mortgage.
    2. Less than 2.5 million yen.
    3. 2.5 million yen or over, but less than 5 million yen.
    4. 5 million yen or over, but less than 7.5 million yen.
    5. 7.5 million yen or over, but less than 10 million yen.
    6. 10 million yen or over, but less than 15 million yen.
    7. 15 million yen or over, but less than 20 million yen.
    8. 20 million yen or over, but less than 30 million yen.
    9. Over 30 million yen.

32. With whom do you live at present? Choose the one that applies (choose only one) from the list below. If you live with someone who are in a de facto state of marriage, assume him or her as a "spouse."

    1. Live alone
    2. Your parent(s)
    3. Your spouse
    4. Your spouse and child(ren) under 18
    5. Your spouse and child(ren) at or over 18
    6. Child(ren) under 18 (No spouse)
    7. Child(ren) at or over 18 (No spouse)
    8. Your spouse and his/her or your parent(s)
    9. Your spouse, his/her or your parent(s), and child(ren) under age 18
    10. Your spouse, his/her or your parent(s), and child(ren) at or over age 18
    11. Friend(s)
    12. Others (Specify)

33. How many people are currently living in your household, including yourself? Please write specific numbers.
34. We would like to ask you about the dependents of your family. Here, a dependent (one supported) is claimed as such on your last tax return. You are …

    1. Supporting someone in your family
    2. Supported by someone in your family
    3. Neither supported nor supporting (single-person households included)

35. How would you describe your current health status?

    1. Excellent
    2. Very good
    3. Good
    4. Fair
    5. Poor

36. Please indicate your highest level of education completed. If you are still in school, select the one you are in now.

    1. Graduated from elementary/junior high school
    2. Graduated from high school
    3. Graduated from college – Associate's Degree (2 years)
    4. Graduated from university – Bachelor's Degree (4 years)
    5. Graduated from graduate school – Doctoral Degree

37. What is your labor union membership status? Choose the one that applies from the list below.

    1. In a labor union at your workplace.
    2. In a labor union not at your workplace.
    3. Not participating in a labor union.
    4. Unknown/unsure.

38. We would like to ask you about your comments. If you have more than one job, please choose one main job. Choose the one that applies from the list below.

    1. Self-employed
    2. Regular employment
    3. Non-regular employment
    4. Dispatched worker
    5. Public servant
    6. Other
    7. In the middle of job seeking
    8. Unemployed

Appendix B
Each Item of the Second Survey

This questionnaire aims to survey opinions on Japan's tax policy and the financial conditions of the Japanese government. We would appreciate it if you answer all the questions, though you may feel some of them are a little bit technical.

We will use these results solely for academic research. Furthermore, since all the results are anonymous, your personal information will be kept confidential.

Thank you very much for your cooperation.

1. GDP measures a society's total income and its total expenditure on newly produced goods and services.[1] Meanwhile, there is an indicator called the long-term debt outstanding of central and local governments (hereafter, long-term government debt). To capture the financial conditions, we often use the $\frac{\text{long-term government debt}}{GDP}$ GDP by considering these two indicators.
   At the end of Fiscal Year (hereafter FY) 1998, the $\frac{\text{long-term government debt}}{GDP}$ in Japan was 105%. This means that the Japanese government owed a little bit more than the country produced in that year.
   How large do you think the $\frac{\text{long-term government debt}}{GDP}$ was at the end of FY 2018? Please fill out your answers in the brackets below.

%

2. The next figure indicates the $\frac{\text{long-term government debt}}{GDP}$ in Japan at the end of FY 1998 and the end of FY 2018, respectively.

[1] The definition of GDP follows Mankiw (2019).

T. Miyazaki et al., *Tax Morale and Tax Resistance*, Kobe University Social Science Research Series, https://doi.org/10.1007/978-981-19-0478-3

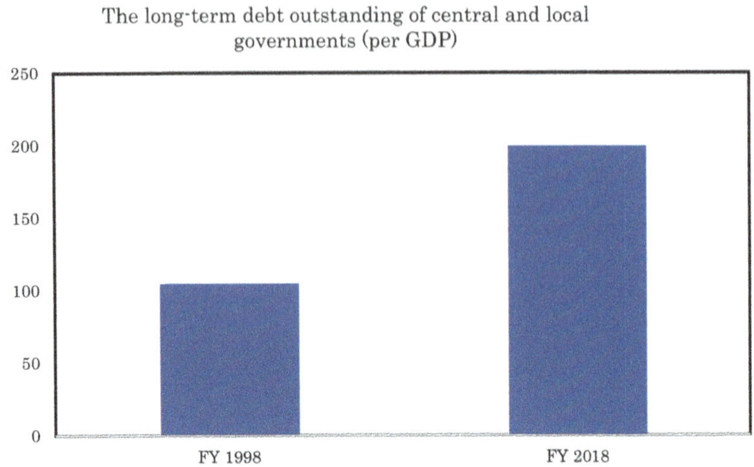

This means that the Japanese government owed about twice what the country produced in one year at the end of FY 2018.
Do you think the Japanese government should reduce government debt, keep the amount of debt at the current level, or incur additional debts?

Reduce debt
Keep debt at the current level
No need to reduce and incur additional debt

3. The following question is only applicable if you chose "reduce public debt" in Question 2. Assume that you could choose between three options for public debt reduction (suppose that the government debt amount is illustrated by the box shown below. The smaller the number of boxes, the smaller the size of the debt reduction; the more the number of boxes, the larger the size of the debt reduction).
Option A: Debt reduction is distributed evenly over the future; that is, **in each year, the same amount of debt is reduced**.

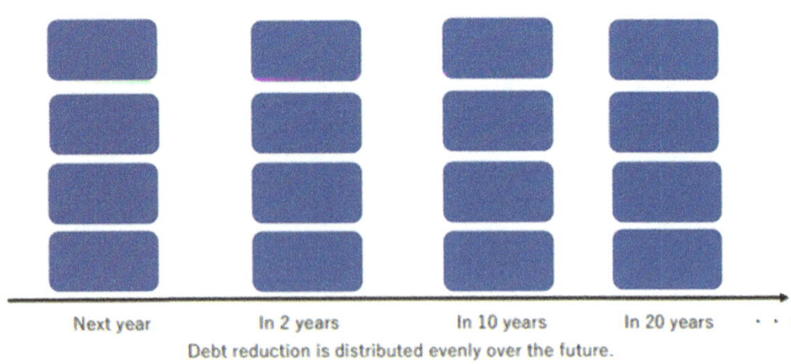

Option B: The extent of debt reduction increases gradually; that is, **in the near future** (e.g., one or two years ahead), **a smaller part of the debt is reduced**, and **in the far future** (ten to 20 years ahead), **a larger part of the debt is reduced**.

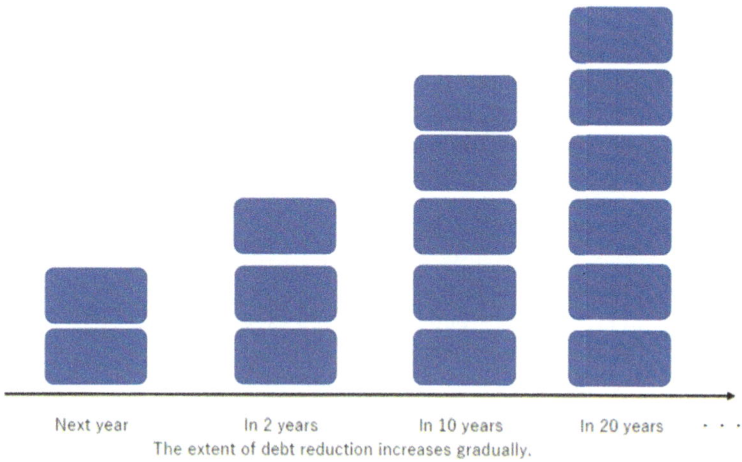

Option C: The extent of debt reduction decreases gradually; that is, **in the near future** (e.g., one or two years ahead), **a larger part of the debt is reduced**, and **in the far future** (ten to 20 years ahead), **a smaller part of the debt will be reduced**.

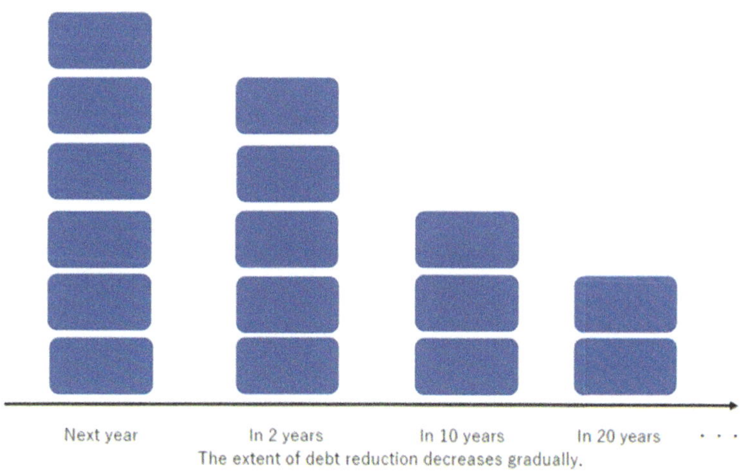

Which of the below options would you choose?

Option A: In each year, the same amount of debt should be reduced

Option B: In the near future, a smaller part of the debt should be reduced. In the future, a larger part of debt should be reduced
Option C: In the near future, a larger part of the debt should be reduced. In the far future, a smaller part of debt should be reduced
N.A.

4. The following question is only applicable if you chose "reduce public debt" in Question 2. What should the government do to reduce government debt? Please choose what you think the government should do. If you think only one item should be cut, please select that item (and move on to the next question). If you want to choose multiple items, please answer in order; all you have to do is to mark the items that should be cut.

   Consumption tax hike
   Cut spending on social security expenditures
   Cut local allocation tax
   Cut spending on public education expenditures
   Cut spending on public work
   Cut spending on national defense expenditures
   Others (you can write what you think the government should reduce)

5. [Please answer this question if you were in such a situation.]
   Please state whether you think the following statement can always be justified, never justified, or something in between: (…) Cheating on tax if you have the chance.
   ("never justified" – code 1 from a ten-point scale, where 1 = never and 10 = always).
6. Do you think your current income tax liability is high?

   1. Low
   2. Slightly low
   3. Appropriate
   4. Slightly higher
   5. High
   6. Not paying income tax

7. Do you think the consumption tax you are paying is high?

   1. Low
   2. Slightly low
   3. Appropriate
   4. Slightly higher
   5. High

8. We may have to discuss whether our consumption tax rate will increase or decrease in the future. What do you think the rate should be? Please answer using the following figure.

		%

9. Our government adopted a reduced consumption tax rate on daily necessities after the standard consumption tax rate increased to 10%. Do you agree with this reduced consumption tax?

    1. Oppose
    2. Somewhat oppose
    3. Neutral
    4. Somewhat supportive
    5. Supportive

10. Some people propose a temporary consumption tax cut to stimulate the economy until the coronavirus is contained. Some countries, such as Germany, have implemented this policy. What do you think about this policy?

    1. We should not reduce the consumption tax rate at all.
    2. We should reduce the tax rate from 10 to 8%.
    3. We should reduce the tax rate from 10 to 5%.
    4. The tax rate should be reduced to below 5%, including the temporary suspension.

11. The government has allocated 140 trillion yen to tackle the coronavirus in the first and second supplementary budgets of FY 2020, approved in April and June, respectively. To execute these budgets, however, the government must issue additional bonds worth 48 trillion yen. What do you think about the size of these economic stimulus packages?

    1. Too small
    2. A little too small
    3. Appropriate size
    4. A little too big
    5. Too big

12. Universal basic income is a government-guaranteed payment that each citizen receives every month, regardless of income, wealth, and job status. The government provides sufficient coverage of the basic cost of living through this program. It is quite similar to the special cash payment for coronavirus relief in that the government gives citizens a certain amount of money. If this system was established, the government would have to take measures, such as the reduction or elimination of social expenditures or tax increases. Do you agree with the introduction of the basic income system in Japan in the future?

    1. Disagree
    2. Somewhat disagree
    3. Neither
    4. Somewhat agree
    5. Agree

13. The following question only applies if you chose "Agree" or "Somewhat agree" in Question 12. How much do you think is necessary? Please choose the amounts for adults and children, respectively.
    Amount for Adults
    1. Less than JPY 50,000
    2. JPY 50,000 or more to less than JPY 100,000
    3. JPY 100,000 or more to less than JPY 150,000
    4. JPY 150,000 or more to less than JPY 200,000
    5. More than JPY 200,000

    Amount for children
    1. Less than JPY 10,000
    2. JPY 10,000 or more to less than JPY 30,000
    3. JPY 30,000 or more to less than JPY 60,000
    4. JPY 60,000 or more to less than JPY 90,000
    5. More than JPY 90,000
14. The following question only applies if the respondent chooses "Agree" or "Somewhat agree" in Question 12. As Question 12 asks, if the basic income system was established, the government would have to take measures such as the reduction or elimination of social expenditures or tax increases. Please choose what you think the government should choose. If you think only one item should be chosen, please select that item only (and move on to the next question). If you have multiple items, please answer in order; simply choose the items that should be chosen.

    Tax increase
    Reduction or abolition of public pensions
    Reduction or abolition of public long-term care insurance
    Reduction or abolition of public medical insurance
    Reduction or abolition of public assistance
    Other (free description)
15. Many jobs will be lost in the future owing to the development of artificial intelligence (AI). What do you think about this opinion?
    1. Agree
    2. Somewhat agree
    3. Neither
    4. Somewhat disagree
    5. Disagree
16. After the coronavirus outbreak subsided, do you think that automation of production systems will be promoted further than ever before, both at home and abroad?
    1. Most likely

2. Likely
3. Neither
4. Less likely
5. Unlikely

17. How often do you use the following media to obtain economic and financial information?

    1. Always
    2. Often
    3. Sometimes
    4. Rarely
    5. Never

    - Newspapers (including electronic media)
    - Television
    - Radio
    - Internet news (e.g. Yahoo and MSN news)
    - Politicians' blogs and Twitter
    - Economist blogs and Twitter
    - Blogs and Twitter of cultural figures, commentators, celebrities, etc.
    - Magazine (including electronic media)
    - Books (including electronic media)
    - Other

18. Businesses are exempt from consumption tax liability in a taxable period if their taxable sales during the base period are less than or equal to 10 million yen. This is the consumption tax exemption threshold system for businesses. Do you recognize this system?

    1. Yes 2. No

19. The amount of consumption tax to be paid for businesses is obtained by deducting the amount of consumption tax on taxable purchases from the amount of consumption tax on taxable sales during the taxable period; that is, the consumption tax on taxable sales minus the consumption tax on taxable purchases is the amount of consumption tax to be paid. Businesses must accurately grasp payable consumption tax. Those with taxable sales of less than or equal to 50 million yen during a base period can simply calculate the amount of tax to be paid from taxable sales. Business entities must submit an application to apply the simplified tax system. This is a simplified consumption tax system. Do you recognize this system?

    1. Yes 2. No

20. To what extent do you trust each of the following from A to C?

(1. Extremely trust, 2. Rather trust, 3. Neither trust nor mistrust, 4. Rather mistrust, 5. Mistrust)

A. Central administrative office	1	2	3	4	5
B. National Diet members	1	2	3	4	5
C. Local assembly members	1	2	3	4	5

21. How much do you agree with the following opinions from A to C? Please state your level of agreement using a scale of 1 (disagree) to 5 (agree).

    A. Civilians cannot influence a government.
    B. Government activities and politics are complicated; thus, people do not understand them.
    C. Your vote is too small to influence the election results because many people vote in the election.
    D. Roughly speaking, it seems National Diet members do not attempt to care for their constituents after their election win.

22. Please choose which of the following political parties you support.

    1. Liberal Democratic Party
    2. Constitutional Democratic Party of Japan
    3. Democratic Party for the People
    4. Japan Innovation Party
    5. Komeito
    6. Japanese Communist Party
    7. Social Democratic Party
    8. Other political parties in Japan ()
    9. Unaffiliated voters

23. How much do you worry about your future life from a financial perspective? Choose the one which applies from the list below.

    1. Strongly agree
    2. Agree a little
    3. Neither
    4. Disagree a little
    5. Strongly disagree
    6. Unknown/unsure

24. Suppose current Japanese society is divided into ten tiers. Which tier currently applies to you? Choose the one that applies from the list below:

1	2	3	4	5	6	7	8	9	10
Highest									Lowest

25. What was the sum of you and your partner's pre-tax income in 2019? Please choose the closest option as follows. If you obtained bonuses other than monthly salaries, please include them in the calculation. If you are a student, please consider the income from a part-time job, allowance from your parents, scholarship, and so forth. Please choose the most appropriate option in the following section.

1. None.
2. Less than 1 million yen.
3. 1 million yen or over, but less than 2 million yen.
4. 2 million yen or over, but less than 4 million yen.
5. 4 million yen or over, but less than 6 million yen.
6. 6 million yen or over, but less than 8 million yen.
7. 8 million yen or over, but less than 10 million yen.
8. 10 million yen or over, but less than 12 million yen.
9. 12 million yen or over, but less than 14 million yen.
10. 14 million yen or over, but less than 16 million yen.
11. 16 million yen or over, but less than 18 million yen.
12. 18 million yen or over, but less than 20 million yen.
13. 20 million yen or over, but less than 22 million yen.
14. Over 22 million yen.
15. Not applicable.

26. What is the total value of your household's financial assets (e.g., bank deposits, stocks, and insurance)? If you are a student, please consider those your parents hold. Choose the one that applies from the list below.

1. Less than 2.5 million yen.
2. 2.5 million yen or over, but less than 5 million yen.
3. 5 million yen or over, but less than 7.5 million yen.
4. 7.5 million yen or over, but less than 10 million yen.
5. 10 million yen or over, but less than 15 million yen.
6. 15 million yen or over, but less than 20 million yen.
7. 20 million yen or over, but less than 30 million yen.
8. 30 million yen or over, but less than 50 million yen.
9. 50 million yen or over, but less than 100 million yen.
10. Over 100 million yen.
11. Unknown/unsure.

27. Do you have to pay off loans? Include all debts, such as home mortgages, car loans, and loans for education.

Yes, I have to pay off mortgages. → Go to Question 28.
No, I do not have to pay off any mortgages. → Go to Questions 29 and 30.

28. Do you have loans other than home mortgages? If so, choose the outstanding amount that applies from the list below. Include all types of loans from which you have to pay interest accrued.

1. No loans other than mortgage.
2. Less than 2.5 million yen.
3. 2.5 million yen or over, but less than 5 million yen.
4. 5 million yen or over, but less than 7.5 million yen.
5. 7.5 million yen or over, but less than 10 million yen.
6. 10 million yen or over, but less than 15 million yen.
7. 15 million yen or over, but less than 20 million yen.
8. 20 million yen or over, but less than 30 million yen.
9. Over 30 million yen.

29. How would you describe your current health status?

    1. Excellent
    2. Very good
    3. Good
    4. Fair
    5. Poor

30. We would like to ask you about your comments. If you have more than one job, please choose one main job. Choose the one that applies from the list below.

    1. Self-employed
    2. Regular employment
    3. Non-regular employment
    4. Dispatched worker
    5. Public servant
    6. Other
    7. In the middle of job seeking
    8. Unemployed

The manufacturer's authorised representative in the EU is Springer Nature Customer Service Centre GmbH, Europaplatz 3, 69115 Heidelberg, Germany. If you have any concerns regarding our products, please contact ProductSafety@springernature.com

Printed and bound by CPI Group (UK) Ltd, Croydon, CR0 4YY
30/09/2026
02225261-0001